GW00503487

Bee Three Publishing is an imprint of Books By Boxer
Published by
Books By Boxer, Leeds, LS13 4BS UK
Books by Boxer (EU), Dublin D02 P593 IRELAND
© Books By Boxer 2023
All Rights Reserved
MADE IN CHINA
ISBN: 9781915410368

MIX
Paper
FSC FSC™ C007683

This book is produced from responsibly sourced paper to ensure forest management

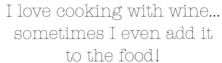

I STARTED MY

Fruit

Juice

DIET
TODAY.

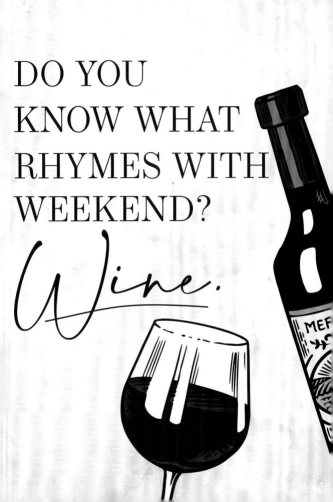

DO YOU KNOW WHAT RHYMES WITH WEEKEND?

Wine.

YOU CAN'T BUY

Happiness,

BUT YOU CAN BUY

Wine

AND THAT'S
KIND OF THE
SAME THING.

MY DOCTOR TOLD ME TO

Watch

MY DRINKING - SO I'VE
STARTED DRINKING IN
FRONT OF THE

Mirror!

KEEP YOUR
Friends
CLOSE BUT YOUR
Wine
CLOSER.

MERL

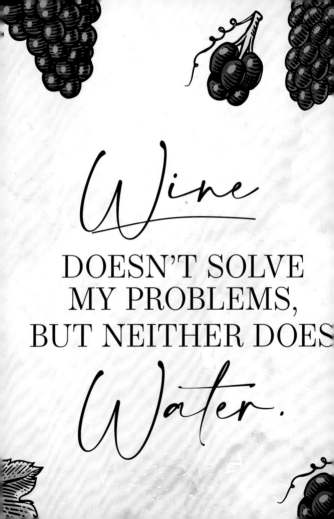

I THINK I
MAY **NEED**
PROFESSIONAL
HELP...
A CHEF, BUTLER
AND MAID
SHOULD DO IT.

I JUST RESCUED SOME

Wine.

IT WAS TRAPPED
IN A BOTTLE.

YOU CAN'T MAKE

Everyone

HAPPY, YOU ARE **NOT** A BOTTLE OF

Wine.

YOU HAD ME AT

Merlot.

MERLOT

ITALIAN

· 1968 ·

I'VE GOT **99** **PROBLEMS** BUT I'M GOING TO DRINK THIS WINE AND IGNORE THEM ALL.

I'M ON A

Champagne

DIET.

TO DO LIST:
Buy *wine*.
Open *wine*.
Pour *wine*.
Drink *wine*.

I'VE NEVER BEEN
A MILLIONAIRE,
BUT I *Know*
I WOULD BE
FABULOUS AT IT.

Beauty

COMES IN ALL SHAPES
AND SIZES.

RED, WHITE, PINK…

Wine

IS THE ANSWER.
I JUST DON'T
REMEMBER THE

Question.

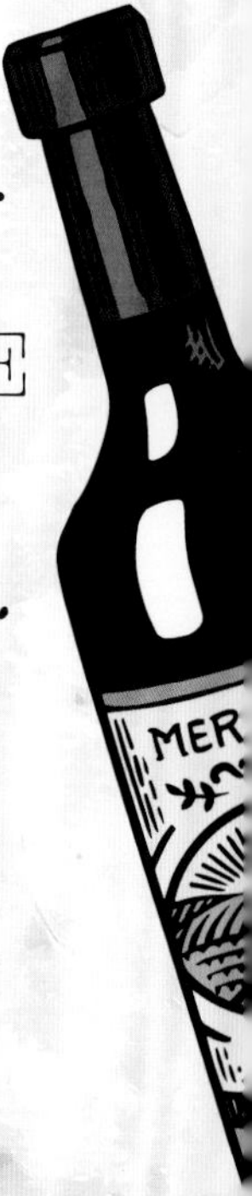

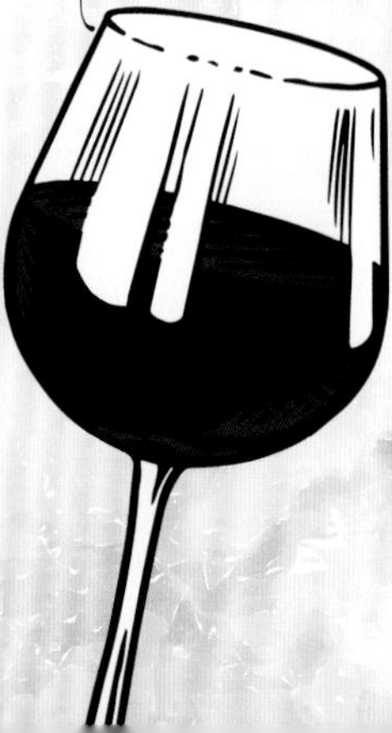

I AM FLUENT IN THESE LANGUAGES: ENGLISH, SARCASM AND PROFANITY.

THE KEY TO LEARNING ABOUT

Wine

IS IN THE DRINKING.

I CALL THIS
Liquid
PATIENCE.

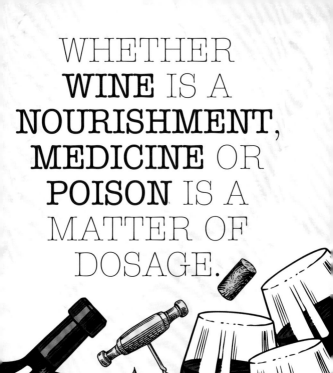

WHETHER **WINE** IS A **NOURISHMENT,** **MEDICINE** OR **POISON** IS A MATTER OF DOSAGE.

I ONLY DRINK

ON DAYS THAT END
WITH A "Y."

MY ONLY
REGRET IN LIFE
IS THAT I DIDN'T
DRINK ENOUGH

Champagne.

AGE AND GLASSES OF

Wine,

SHOULD NEVER BE COUNTED.

MERLOT

ITALIAN

· 1968 ·

Wine.

JUICE WITH MORE LIFE EXPERIENCE.

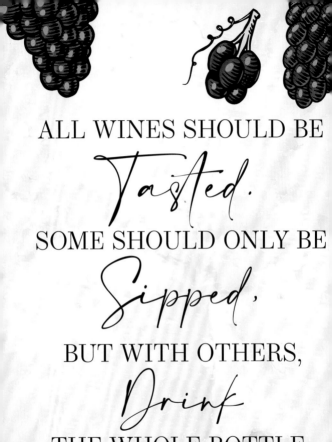

ALL WINES SHOULD BE

Tasted.

SOME SHOULD ONLY BE

Sipped,

BUT WITH OTHERS,

Drink

THE WHOLE BOTTLE.

Wine

IS, PERHAPS, THE
CLOSEST THING THE
PLANET HAS TO AN

Elixir of Life.

LIFE'S TOO

Short

TO DRINK BAD

Wine!

TRUST ME - THE WINE SAID I **CAN** DANCE!

I FIND THE MOST **IMPORTANT** TOOL IN THE KITCHEN IS A **CORKSCREW.**

I'M ONE GLASS OF

Wine

FROM TELLING YOU WHAT

I really THINK.

ALEXA,
POUR MORE
Wine!